WARBIRDS ILLUSTRATED NO. 7

Cover illustration: A Jaguar GR.1 of 14 Sqn., RAF Germany. (MJG)

1. The General Dynamics F-16 will over the coming years become the basic combat aircraft of several NATO countries. The aircraft depicted here is an F-16 of the Royal Norwegian Air Force. (GD)

WARBIRDS ILLUSTRATED NO. 7

NATO Air Power in the 1980s

Belgium ● Canada ● Denmark ● France ● West Germany
Greece ● Italy ● Netherlands ● Norway ● Portugal ● Spain
Turkey ● United Kingdom ● United States

MICHAEL J. GETHING

a&ap

ARMS AND ARMOUR PRESS
London—Melbourne—Harrisburg, Pa.

Introduction

Warbird 7: NATO Air Power in the 1980s
Published in 1982 by
Arms and Armour Press, Lionel Leventhal Limited,
2–6 Hampstead High Street, London NW3 1QQ;
4–12 Tattersalls Lane, Melbourne, Victoria 3000,
Australia; Cameron and Kelker Streets, P.O. Box 1831,
Harrisburg, Pennsylvania 17105, U.S.A.

British Library Cataloguing in Publication Data:
Gething, M. J.
NATO Air Power in the 1980s. – (Warbirds
illustrated; 7)
1. North Atlantic Treaty Organization
2. Aeroplanes, Military – Pictorial works
I. Title   II. Series
623.74'6'091821   UG1240
ISBN 0-85368-545-2

Layout by Anthony A. Evans.
Printed in Great Britain by William Clowes
(Beccles) Limited.

The air forces of the NATO alliance enter the 1980s with a much-needed boost from two quarters: many of those air forces are introducing new types of aircraft; and Spain has been formally invited to join in the alliance. After a period during the 1970s when many of the NATO allies were allocating their defence budgets in directions other than aviation, the second half of this decade will see the NATO air forces better able to meet the Warsaw Pact threat.

The re-equipment programmes that will have the most impact on the ability of NATO air forces to meet this threat are the General Dynamics F-16 Fighting Falcon, which is to be supplied to Belgium, Denmark, Norway, the Netherlands and USAF Europe; the Panavia Tornado, the interdictor-strike version of which is to enter service in Germany, Italy and the UK, and the air defence variant (the F.2) intended for the RAF; the Dassault-Breguet Mirage 2000, due to enter French service in the mid-1980s; and the NATO-owned fleet of Boeing E-3A Sentry airborne early warning aircraft. This last project is an innovative one for NATO: the E-3A fleet will be funded by NATO and operated by multinational crews. Although their main base will be at Gielenkirchen in Germany, the aircraft will operate from various forward operating bases, in NATO insignia. Together with the RAF's British Aerospace Nimrod AEW.3, they will offer increased warning time of hostile actions and, in the event of hostilities, will enhance the effectiveness of NATO air power. Spain has yet to join the alliance formally, but it is only a matter of time before this is officially concluded. Indeed, by the time this book appears, Spain could well be a bona fide member – hence her inclusion in this volume. By the same token, France is also included, as, although no longer in the military command of NATO, she has not formally left the alliance.

The photographs in this book have been drawn from many sources, including the air arms themselves, the aircraft manufacturers and my own collection. To the many people who have contributed, I offer my thanks. In the space available, I have concentrated on combat aircraft and tactical support transports and helicopters; while situations in some countries have made it difficult to obtain photographs of certain types, despite several avenues of approach. However, it is, I believe, an interesting selection of the major types in service, or about to enter service with NATO air arms during this decade. They can be seen at most of the air shows open to the public across NATO Europe, or in the skies above these nations.

Michael J. Gething, Farnborough, 1982.

2. The only NATO-owned aircraft within the alliance – the Boeing E-3A Sentry AWACS (airborne warning and control system). A fleet of 18 aircraft are being procured to provide NATO with an early warning force. The member nations have contributed a proportion of the E-3A's costs. The fitting out of the avionics is being supervised by Dornier in Germany after delivery from Boeing. When fully operational, the NATO E-3A Sentry will use Gielenkirchen in Germany as their main base, but detachments will be located at forward operating bases on the flanks of NATO. The NATO E-3A will be fully inter-operable with the RAF's Nimrod AEW.3 fleet. (Boeing)

◀2

▲3

3. The Belgian Air Force, along with those of the Netherlands, Denmark and Norway, will have the General Dynamics F-16 as its main combat aircraft in the 1980s. This F-16 was one of the first batch to equip 1 Wing of the Belgian Air Force. 349 Sqn. of 1 Wing was the first F-16 unit in NATO to be declared operational, on 1 January 1981. It was followed by 350 Sqn. of 1 Wing. The two F-104G units of 10 Wing (23 and 31 Sqns.) are due to be equipped with the F-16 by August 1983. (General Dynamics)

4. The F-104G Starfighter has been the mainstay of Belgium's air force since the mid-1960s. It will remain in service until re-equipment with the F-16 is completed in mid-1983. This aircraft

of 10 Wing is shown with wing-tip and underwing fuel tanks. (AFCENT)

5. The Belgian Air Force complemented their F-104G fleet with the Dassault-Breguet Mirage 5 in 1970; in all, some 63 5BA fighter-bombers (an example of which is shown), plus 27 5BR reconnaissance and 16 5BD trainer versions. (AFCENT)

6. The Dassault-Breguet/Dornier Alpha Jet is the basic and advanced jet trainer of the Belgian Air Force. Belgium became the third country (after France and Germany) to select the aircraft, the first of 33 Alpha Jet 1Bs for Belgium flying in 1978. In this flight-line shot at St. Truiden, the aircraft are configured with reusable rocket pods for weapons training. (AMD-BA)

▼4

5▲ 6▼

9▲

7. Until the arrival of the CF-18 Hornets in the late-1980s, the Canadair/Lockheed CF-104G Starfighter will remain the mainstay of the 1st Canadian Air Group in Europe, based at Baden-Soellingen, Germany. This photograph shows an aircraft of 441 Sqn. at RAF Wildenrath during the Tactical Weapons Meet in 1978. (MJG)

8. Although not based in Europe, the Canadian Armed Force's Canadair/Northrop CF-5A fighters are assigned to SACEUR (Supreme Allied Commander Europe) for deployment in Norway in an emergency. Here, a CF-5A is receiving fuel from an RAF Victor K.2 tanker aircraft. (MoD-Air)

9. The 1st Canadian Air Group is supported by two de Havilland Aircraft of Canada CC-132 Dash-7 transports delivered in 1979. The two aircraft are operated by 412 Sqn., based at Lahr in Germany. (DHC)

10. Liaison in 1CAG is provided by some eleven Bell CH-136 Kiowa (military JetRanger) helicopters of 444 Sqn., also based at Lahr. (MJG)

10▼

▲11 ▼12

11. Denmark, one of the four countries in Europe to procure the General Dynamics F-16, now has two squadrons (727 and 730 Esk) equipped with the aircraft. (General Dynamics)

12. Denmark was the first overseas customer for the SAAB J35 Draken, procuring 46 aircraft in three versions – the F-35 fighter-bomber, the RF-35 reconnaissance aircraft and the TF-35 trainer – in 1970–71. The aircraft illustrated is an RF-35, with an FFV Red Baron IR-scanner recce pod under the wing. (FFV)

13. Although receiving F-16s, Denmark will continue to operate Starfighters into the 1980s. This photograph shows an F-104G of 726 Esk in a heavily weathered dark green overall camouflage scheme. Note the launch rails for AIM-9 Sidewinder air-to-air missiles on the fuselage undersurface aft of the nose-wheel door. Note the two-seat TF-104G in the background. (MJG)

14. Apart from using the SAAB T-17 Supporter for basic pilot training by her air force, the Danish Army flies the type as an airborne observation post. (SAAB-Scania)

▲15 ▼16

15. A flight of three Mirage IIIEs using their booster rockets in a climb to height. Although dating back to the late-1960s, the Mirage IIIE is still a major part of the French Tactical Air Command.

16. Other Mirage III versions still in service are the IIIR/RD reconnaissance variants. This photograph shows a Mirage IIIRD (an R version with IIIE avionics) of ER 33 based at Strasbourg. A reconnaissance version of the Mirage F1, the F1CR, is due to begin replacing the IIIR/RDs from late 1983 onwards. (AMD-BA)

17. The airborne arm of the French strategic nuclear deterrent, Le Force de Frappe, is equipped with the Mirage IVA bomber. Some 15-20 aircraft are currently being updated to ensure an airborne component until the arrival of the Mirage 2000N in the late 1980s. (SIRPA)

20▲

18, 19. After the refusal to supply the Mirage 5F to Israel in the late 1960s, France bought back the aircraft and put them into L'Armee de l'Air service. **18.** An aircraft of EC 13 based at Colmar, prior to camouflage being introduced in the late 1970s. (SIRPA) **19.** A Mirage 5 with the camouflage applied. (MJG) **20.** A Mirage F1C armed with two close-combat Matra 550

'Magic' air-to-air missiles on the outer wing and two of the larger and longer range Matra Super 530 air-to-air missiles on the inner wing pylons.
21. The Mirage 2000 is shortly to enter service as an interceptor, complementing (and later replacing) the F1C force in French service. (AMD-BA)

21▼

▲22
22. Like the RAF, the French ordered 200 Jaguars for use by their Tactical Air Command. This photograph shows a two-seat Jaguar E taking on fuel from a C-135F Stratotanker, while the single-seat Jaguar A formates on the two. Note the centreline fuel tank and the underwing rocket pod on the Jaguar A. (SIRPA)

23. Although the AMD-BA/Dornier Alpha Jet 1E procured by the French is ostensibly for use as an advanced jet trainer, its employment as a close support aircraft by the Germans could well mean that French Alpha Jets would assume a similar role in the event of a European war. The aircraft shown belongs to

▼23

GE.314. EC.8, the weapons training unit and squadron most likely to use the Alpha Jet 'in anger' were scheduled to receive their aircraft in 1982. (AMD-BA)

24. A General Dynamics F-16A of the Royal Netherlands Air Force, armed with two AIM-9 Sidewinder air-to-air missiles, supplemented by an internally mounted 20mm Vulcan cannon. (GD)

25. The F1C-200 version of the Mirage F1C, which replaced the Mirage IIICs in use as interceptors during the 1970s. The F1C-200 pictured belongs to EC5, based at Orange, and features a nose-mounted in-flight refuelling probe. (AMD-BA)

▲26 ▼27

26. The remaining F-104G units of the West German Air Force will be progressively equipped with the Panavia Tornadoes from 1983 onwards. This example of the German pre-series aircraft (PS.11) is carrying the MBB MW-1 airfield denial weapon, with which some units will be equipped. (MBB)

27. The Spanish Navy's air arm operates one squadron (Esc.008) of British Aerospace AV-8A Harriers, known as AV-8S Matadors, from their carrier *Dedalo*. Here an AV-8S is seen on *Dedalo*, with a two-seat TAV-8S behind it. Eleven AV-8Ss and two TAV-8Ss were delivered. (via the Spanish Navy)

28. The first of the second batch of Transall C-160 transports currently being built to replace the Noratlas transports remaining in French service. Built jointly by Aérospatiale and MBB/VFW, 25 C-160s are under construction, 15 of which will have the in-flight refuelling equipment illustrated. The new C-160s will equip ETs.63 and 64 in 1983. (Aérospatiale)

29. Although not strictly combat aircraft, there are eleven Boeing C-135F Stratotankers in French service. Their prime role is to support the Mirage IV fleet, with secondary support of overseas deployments of French air power. Here, a C-135F refuels a Mirage F1C-200. (AMD-BA)

28▲ 29▼

30. A Super Etendard of L'Aéronavale being launched. France is one of the few remaining countries to possess a conventional fixed-wing carrier aviation element. Some 71 aircraft are to be delivered, replacing not only the older Etendards but also the F-8E(FN) Crusaders. (AMD-BA)

31. The other fixed-wing element of L'Aéronavale is the Breguet Br.1050 Alize, 28 of which are being updated with Iguane radar, Omega navigation and ESM (Electronic Support Measures) for anti-submarine warfare (ASW) duties. This photograph shows an Alize landing on *Clemenceau*. (SIRPA)

32. The French Navy's shore-based ASW force is to re-equip with 42 new-build Atlantic maritime patrol aircraft from 1986. This is the first prototype Atlantic Nouvelle Generation, converted from an existing Atlantic. (AMD-BA)

33. As part of the Anglo-French helicopter deal of the mid-1960s, the French Navy is taking some 40 Westland/Aérospatiale Lynx ASW helicopters to operate from her destroyers. Unlike the Royal Navy's Lynx HAS.2, the French Navy Lynx is equipped with an Alcatel DUAV.4 lightweight dunking sonar. This unusual photograph shows a Lynx being winched into the hangar of the French guided-missile destroyer *Georges Leygues*. (ECP-Armées)

▲34

▲35 ▼36

34. The French Army aviation element, ALAT (Aviation Légère de l'Armée de Terre) is now the world's third largest helicopter operator. One of their Aérospatiale SA342M Gazelles is seen here launching its Euromissile HOT (Haut subsonique Optiquement téléguidé tiré d'un Tube) anti-armour missile at low-level. (Euromissile)

35. 'Now you see me . . .' An Aérospatiale SA341F Gazelle light observation helicopter, equipped with an Athos sight, uses nap-of-the-earth flying techniques to reduce visual detection on reconnaissance missions. (Aérospatiale)

36. An Aérospatiale SA330B Puma dropping a French Army Milan anti-tank guided weapon team. Unlike the British, who have the RAF fly their Puma helicopters in support of the Army, ALAT fly their own Pumas. (Euromissile)

37. The Lockheed F-104G Starfighter was the mainstay of the Luftwaffe during the late 1960s and throughout the 1970s. It remains in service with four fighter-bomber wings, but is due to be replaced by the Tornado IDS variant. A Starfighter pilot of JBG 33 is seen here preparing for a sortie during a NATO weapons meet. (MJG)

38. The Luftwaffe took delivery of their McDonnell Douglas F-4F Phantoms during 1972–73, following the success of the RF-4E reconnaissance versions. Two air defence wings (JG 71 and JG 74) and two ground attack wings (JBG 35 and JBG 36) were equipped from the 175 aircraft purchased. An F-4F Phantom of JBG 36 is illustrated. The large tail letter on the fin is not usually carried: this being a code used during the Central Region Tactical Air Meet at Wildenrath in 1978. (MJG)

▲39   ▼40

39. The RF-4E version of the Phantom was purchased to replace the RF-104Gs in Luftwaffe service. The first of 88 was delivered in 1971, and the type equips AG 51 and AG 52 based at Leck. In the late 1970s/early 1980s, the 81 remaining aircraft were modified with weapons pylons to enable them to perform a tactical bombing secondary role. This aircraft of AG 52 has been so modified; note the inner weapons pylon absent from the aircraft as delivered. (MJG)

40. Tornadoes from RAF Cottesmore, where aircrew of the three nations that developed the aircraft receive their training. (RAF)

41. An early pre-production Tornado in Bundesmarine markings, carrying four Kormoran anti-shipping missiles. The Bundes-marine will eventually receive 120 Tornadoes. (Panavia)

42. The Dassault-Breguet/ Dornier Alpha Jet A has replaced the German-built G.91R fighter-bombers in German service. These four aircraft are assigned to JBG 49. Two other Geschwader, JBG 41 and JBG 43, are similarly equipped. (Dornier)

43. Although not possessing aircraft carriers, the German Navy does have a shore-based air arm, the Marinesflieger. Their strike squadrons MFG 1 and 2 will be the first operational units of the three nations to receive the Panavia Tornado later in 1982. A prototype aircraft (P.04) is seen here in Marinesflieger markings with the MFG 1 badge on the fin, armed with four MBB Kormoran anti-ship missiles, outside a hardened aircraft shelter. (MBB)

▲42 ▼43

44. The tactical transport element of the Luftwaffe is provided by the Transall C-160D, built by MBB/VFW in Germany and Aérospatiale in France. Some 110 aircraft were delivered in the late 1960s, and three squadrons, LTG 61, 62 and 63, were equipped with the type. LTG 62, based at Wunsdorf, an example of which is illustrated, also acts as the training unit for the C-160D. (RAF Strike Command)

44 ▲

45. Maritime patrol and long-range ASW work for the Marines-flieger is undertaken by 15 Breguet Br.1150 Atlantic aircraft, originally procured in the mid-1960s, and recently updated to keep pace with the threat during the 1980s. The remaining four aircraft out of the 20 delivered (one having been lost) have been modified for 'Elint' (electronic intelligence) work. *(Bildstelle der Marine)*

46. The German Army's air component, the Heeresflieger, is in the process of receiving the last of 212 MBB Bo.105P (PAH-1) anti-armour helicopters, armed with six Euromissile HOT anti-tank guided weapons. The Heeresflieger is also equipped with the unarmed Bo.105M for the light observation and communications role. (MBB Helicopters)

▲45 ▼46

47▲ 48▼

47. Dornier-built Bell UH-1D Iroquois (now popularly known as 'Hueys') feature strongly in the Heeresflieger inventory. Here, a UH-1D assigned to the ACE (Allied Command Europe) Mobile Force artillery section is seen taking on board Belgian Para-commandos during exercises in Portugal. (Ian V. Hogg)

48. The other major type in Heeresflieger service is the Sikorsky CH-53G, built under licence by VFW-Fokker in Germany. Delivery of 110 CH-53Gs was completed in 1975. This photograph shows a Land Rover and 105mm Light Gun being unloaded during a NATO exercise in Germany. (UKLF)

▲49

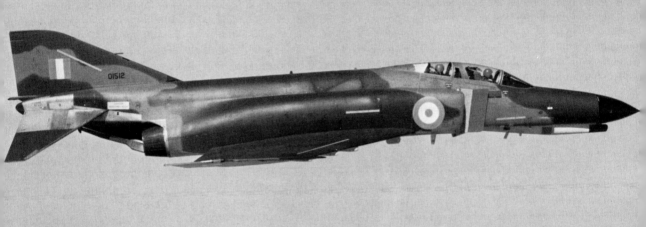

▲50 ▼51

52▲ 53▼

49. One of the 40 Dassault-Breguet Mirage F1CG air superiority fighters supplied to Greece. Delivery was completed in 1977. The Mirage equips two squadrons comprising the 114ª Pterix Mahis based at Tanagra. Their main armament (not shown here) is the Matra R.550 'Magic' air-to-air missile. (AMD-BA)

50. In all, the Hellenic Air Force has received 58 McDonnell Douglas F-4E Phantoms (illustrated), which are used in the air defence and close air support roles. A further eight RF-4E reconnaissance variants are also in Greek service. (McDD)

51. An F-4E of 117 Wing, Hellenic Air Force, seen at Ramstein during the 1980 Tactical Air Meet. (R. L. Ward)

52. To support maritime air operations, the Hellenic Air Force ordered 60 Vought A-7H Corsairs, delivery of which was completed in 1977. In 1978, they ordered six two-seat trainer versions (one of which is illustrated) to supplement the single-seat A-7Hs. The first example was converted from an A-7H, but the remaining five were new-build aircraft. (Vought)

53. This photograph shows a Northrop F-5A of the 111 Pterighe Hellenic Air Force based at Nea Ankhialos. In addition to three squadrons of F-5A day interdiction aircraft, the Hellenic Air Force also has two squadrons of the RF-5A reconnaissance fighter. (Hellenic Air Force)

▲54

54. The Greek Army operates some 40 examples of the Agusta-built version of the Bell UH-1D/H Iroquois, designated AB.205. (Agusta)

55. The Greek Navy operates some 16 AB.212 ASW helicopters,

detached on board her naval vessels. The AB.212 ASW is a licence-built version of the Bell 212, modified for ASW operations. Note the radome over the forward cabin. (Agusta)

▼55

56. A pair of Aeritalia-developed F-104S Starfighters of 21 Gruppo, 53 Stormo, based at Cameri. These versions will remain in Aeronautica Militare Italiano (AMI) service well into the 1990s. (Aeritalia)

57. Italy is to take 100 Panavia Tornadoes into AMI service, beginning later this year. This photograph shows the first Italian-built prototype aircraft P.05, taking off from Casselle. Note the flame cones from the afterburner. (Aeritalia)

56▲ 57▼

▲58

▲59 ▼60

58. The Fiat (now Aeritalia) G.91T advanced trainer (right), in company with a G.91PAN of the Italian aerobatic team 'Frecci Tricolori' (who have now re-equipped with AerMacchi MB.339 trainers). Note the bulged rear canopy to give the instructor a better view. (MJG)

59. In 1968, AMI took delivery of its first G.91Y attack aircraft. This Aeritalia-developed version of the G.91 features a pair of General Electric J85 turbojets in place of the single Bristol Siddeley Orpheus 803 of the G.91R/T. Some 65 aircraft were delivered. This photograph shows an aircraft of 101 Gruppo, 8 Stormo. (Aeritalia)

60. Work is in hand in Italy for a successor to the G.91R/Y and strike versions of the F-104G/S. Aeritalia and AerMacchi are co-operating on the new AM-X, which is due to enter AMI service in 1987. An artist's impression of the proposed aircraft is shown here. Embraer of Brazil have since joined the project, and are expected to produce 80 plus under licence. Italy is expected to have a requirement for over 200 AM-X aircraft. (Aeritalia)

61. A Breguet Br.1150 Atlantic maritime patrol and ASW aircraft of the Royal Netherlands Navy.

62. One of the first of the BAe Nimrod MR.2 maritime patrol and ASW aircraft to be returned to service with an updated avionics and radar fit, designed to keep pace with the Soviet submarine threat into the 1990s. In all, 34 aircraft (all that are available) are being updated to MR.2 standard. Note the revised 'hemp' coloured upper surface camouflage colour, and the 'B' type roundels. (BAe Manchester)

▲63 ▼64

63. The main air defence aircraft of USAF Europe is the McDonnell Douglas F-15 Eagle, armed with four AIM-9 Sidewinders and four AIM-7 Sparrow air-to-air missiles and an internal 20mm Vulcan cannon. The 36th Tactical Fighter Wing (TFW) at Bitburg has 72 F-15C/Ds, while the 32nd TFS based at Soesterburg in the Netherlands has another 18 aircraft. The single-seat F-15C version is illustrated here. (McDonnell Douglas)

64. Although the Tornado is a joint UK/German/Italian venture, the UK is the only nation taking the Air Defence Variant. Here, the third development prototype Tornado F.2 (as the RAF designate the ADV) is seen in the low-visibility 'air superiority grey' camouflage scheme, with toned-down national insignia. This particular aircraft was also the first to be equipped with the Marconi Avionics/Ferranti air intercept radar developed for the Tornado F.2. (BAe Warton)

65. Although possessing a dozen C-130H Hercules, AMI's main tactical transport is the Aeritalia G.222, operated by 46 Brigada. To date, 44 aircraft are on order, although AMI may well procure a further small batch. (Aeritalia)

66. Italy's maritime patrol resources comprise 18 Breguet Br.1150 Atlantics operated by two units of AMI on behalf of and under the control of Marinavia, the naval air arm. (AMD-BA)

67. Marinavia operate some 24 Agusta-built SH-3D Sea Kings from several naval vessels. They are also expected to fly from the helicopter carrier, *Giuseppe Garibaldi*, due to enter service in the mid-1980s. Note the AS-12 missiles mounted outboard of the floats and homing torpedoes inboard. (Agusta)

65 ▲

66 ▲　67 ▼

68. The Italian Army aviation element operate some 24 Boeing Vertol CH-47C Chinook medium-lift helicopters, built under licence by the Meridionali consortium in Italy. (MJG)

69. Another project illustrated by a mock-up is the Agusta A.129 Mangusta attack helicopter. Three prototypes are under construction, powered by the Rolls-Royce Gem engine of the Westland Lynx. The Italian Army hope to order the A.129 in quantity, armed with eight TOW anti-armour missiles. (Agusta)

▲68 ▼69

70▲ 71▼

70. One of the first General Dynamics' F-16A fighters to join the Royal Netherlands Air Force. Initially, 102 aircraft (80 F-16As and 22 F-16B two-seat trainers) were ordered in 1975, but orders for two follow-on batches of 22 and 18 aircraft have been made subsequently, out of a total requirement for 213 needed by 1989. Two units, 322 and 323 Sqns., are operational, while 311 and 312 Sqns. are in the process of converting to the type. (General Dynamics)

71. The first F-16B trainer for the Royal Netherlands Air Force on its maiden flight in June 1979. (General Dynamics)

72. A pair of RF-104G Starfighters of 306 Sqn., RNethAF on the flight line at Wildenrath during the 1978 Tactical Weapons Meet. This squadron will be the last Starfighter unit to convert to the F-16, sometime in 1984. (MJG)

73. The transport needs of the Royal Netherlands Air Force are met by 334 Sqn., based at Soesterberg, equipped with nine Fokker F27M troopships and three F27 Mk.100 VIP transports. (Fokker)

▲72 ▼73

74 ▲ 75 ▼

74. A Canadair/Northrop NF-5A of 316 Sqn., based at Eindhoven, at the 1978 Tactical Weapons Meet. These aircraft differ from the standard F-5A in being fitted with Doppler navigation systems and manoeuvring flaps, similar to those used on the later F-5E. (MJG)

75. One of the 70-odd Aérospatiale Alouette III helicopters used for observation and communications duties by 298 and 299 Sqns. of the Royal Netherlands Air Force on behalf of the Dutch Army. (MJG)

41

▲76 ▼77

76. The Dutch naval air arm, Marine Luchtvaartdienst, operate six Breguet Br.1150 Atlantic maritime patrol and ASW aircraft. They are flown by 321 Sqn., based at Valkenburg. (*Koninklijke Marine*)

77. The first Lockheed P-3C Orion of Marine Luchtvaartdienst on its first flight. There are thirteen aircraft on order, the first of which were delivered early in 1982, to be flown by 320 Sqn. (Lockheed-California)

78. The first General Dynamics F-16s for the Royal Norwegian Air Force entered service in 1980, with 332 Sqn. being the first unit to convert to them. Norway is to receive 60 F-16As and 12 two-seat F-16Bs. Eventually, F-16s will replace the F-104G, CF-104 and F-5A in Norway's inventory. Note the extended fairing above the jet tailpipe on this F-16A: this houses the brake parachute required for operations from Norwegian airfields. (General Dynamics)

79. Two Royal Norwegian Air Force Starfighters at a UK air display in the mid-1970s. The single-seat F-104G (left) and the two-seat TF-104G are from 331 Sqn. based at Bodo. (MJG)

80. Norway has two operational units equipped with the Northrop F-5: 336 Sqn. has the F-5A fighter-bomber, the F-5B trainer and a flight of RF-5A reconnaissance fighters; 338 Sqn. has the F-5A only; while one other unit, 718 Sqn., is equipped with the F-5A and the F-5B for training. An F-5A of 336 Sqn., usually based at Rygge, is seen here at RAF Gutersloh during a NATO exercise. (MJG)

78▲

79▲ 80▼

▲81

▲82

▲83 ▼84

81. The Royal Norwegian Air Force operates seven Lockheed P-3B Orion for coastal and maritime patrol duties. Five were originally delivered in 1969 to 333 Sqn. at Andoya, and a further two were subsequently procured in 1980. (Lockheed-California)

82. One of the six Lockheed C-130H Hercules transports operated by 335 Sqn. This particular aircraft, photographed at RAF Gutersloh in 1981, shows the aircraft operating on behalf of the United Nations. (MJG)

83. The first of six Westland Lynx naval variants ordered for coastguard duties on a test flight in the UK. The Lynx will be flown by 337 Sqn., Royal Norwegian Air Force. (Westland Helicopters)

84. The most recent addition to Portugal's Air Force is the Vought A-7P Corsair. Some 20 aircraft were delivered early in 1982, the first of which is illustrated. The A-7P is an ex-US Navy A-7A refurbished and fitted with more powerful TF30-P-408 engines plus A-7E standard avionics. (Vought)

45

▲85

▲86 ▼87

85. Portugal has received a total of 42 German-built Fiat
G.91R-3/4 fighter-bombers surplus to Luftwaffe requirements.
Since the retirement of the F-86 Sabre interceptor squadron, the
G.91s have been equipped with AIM-9 Sidewinders as an interim
solution. This photograph shows a G.91R3 on an exchange visit
to a French unit. (SIRPA – Air)

86. The Portuguese Air Force operates the C-130H Hercules in
the medium transport role, as depicted here. (Lockheed-Georgia)
87. The Portuguese aerobatic team 'Asas de Portugal' with their
Cessna T-37C trainers. They are part of Esc.102 of Grupo 21
based at Sintra. (MJG)

88. The Dassault-Breguet Mirage F1 was procured by Spain in three versions: the F1CE interceptor, F1BE trainer, and F1EE strike variant. This photograph shows two Mirage F1CEs of Esc.141, based at Los Lianos, taking off on a mission. (AMD-BA)

89. Spain was an early customer for the Dassault-Breguet Mirage IIIE, receiving 24 aircraft, designated IIIEE, and six IIIDE trainers. These are operated by Esc.111 at Manises. (S. Mafé Huertas, via AMD-BA)

88▲ 89▼

▲90

▲91　▼92

90. In 1971–72, the United States supplied Spain with 36 McDonnell Douglas F-4CR(S) Phantoms for interception duties as part payment for base rights in Spain. The F-4CR(S) Phantoms were supplemented by four RF-4Cs delivered in 1978. Both versions are operated by Esc.121. (McDonnell Douglas)

91. The Northrop F-5 was licence-built in Spain by CASA in three versions: the SF-5A, the SRF-5A recce version, and the SF-5B trainer (illustrated). Three units, one training and two operational, are equipped with the type, of which a total of 70 were built. (CASA)

92. CASA's indigenous light transport, the C-212 Aviocar, has been used by the Spanish Air Force in four major versions: the C-212A (T.12B) utility transport (illustrated); the C-212AV VIP transport, of which five are in service; the C-212B (TR.12A) photographic survey version, of which six are in service; and the C-212E navigation trainer, of which five are operated. (MJG)

93. Esc.221 of the Spanish Air Force operates six ex-US Navy Lockheed P-3A Orions for maritime reconnaissance and ASW work. It is possible that since Spain's recent entry into NATO, a further squadron of ex-US P-3A/Bs may be made available. (Lockheed)

94. The Spanish Navy operates one of the world's smallest ASW helicopters from *Dedalo* and other vessels – the Hughes 500M (ASW). In 1972, sixteen were delivered, and the survivors equip Esc.006. Note the magnetic anomaly detector (MAD) drogue offset from the aircraft's starboard side, and the two homing torpedoes under the cabin. (Hughes Helicopters)

95. The heavy transport squadron of the Spanish Army's air component, FAMET (Fuerzas Aero Moviles del Ejército de Tierra) operates twelve Boeing Vertol CH-47C Chinook helicopters from Colmenar Viejo, near Madrid. (Boeing Vertol)

93▲

94▲ 95▼

▲96 ▼97

96. The Turkish Air Force took delivery of 40 Aeritalia F-104S Starfighters in 1976, to supplement the earlier Lockheed F-104Gs in service. In the early eighties, these F-104Gs were gradually replaced by a variety of Dutch, Belgian and West German F-104Gs surplus to requirements, following the arrival of the F-16 and Phantoms in those countries. Our photograph shows a batch of six Turkish F-104S Starfighters ready for delivery at Aeritalia's Casselle airfield. (Aeritalia)

97. Turkey has received a total of 71 McDonnell Douglas F-4E Phantoms (illustrated), together with eight RF-4E versions. A further batch of F-4Es are being delivered from surplus USAF stocks. (McDonnell Douglas)

98. Seven Lockheed C-130E Hercules (uprated to –H standard) have been supplied to Turkey. They equip 222 Filo of Turkish Air Support Command. (via Joint Services Recognition Journal)

99. This photograph shows one of the 20 ex-Luftwaffe C-160 Transall transports passed on to the Turkish Air Force. They are flown by 221 Filo, from the Erkilot/Kayseri Airbase. (via R. L. Ward)

98▲ 99▼

100. The BAC Lightning will remain in RAF service until the mid-1980s, when they will be replaced by the first Tornado F.2s. This photograph shows the three units still flying the type, all based at Binbrook. Nearest the camera is a Lightning T.5 of the Lightning Training Flight, then comes an F.6 of 11 Sqn., with an F.6 of 5 Sqn. farthest from the camera. (MoD-Air)

101. The McDonnell Douglas Phantom is the mainstay of the RAF's air defence force. They fly two versions: the F-4K/FG.1 (originally procured for the Fleet Air Arm) and the F-4M/FGR.2. Deployed in the UK and Germany, altogether there are seven squadrons equipped with the type. This Phantom FGR.2 of 19 Sqn., based at RAF Wildenrath, is armed with four AIM-9 Sidewinder AAMs, four BAeD SkyFlash AAMs and one 20mm Vulcan SUU/23 gun pod. Note the fin-top fairing for the radar warning receiver. (MoD-RAFG)

102. To replace the rapidly-ageing Shackleton AEW.2 radar-warning aircraft of 8 Sqn., the RAF are in the process of receiving eleven Nimrod AEW.3 airborne early warning aircraft, converted from MR.1 airframes. The main differences are the two bulbous radomes on the nose and tail, the Loral ESM pods on the wing-tips, and an internal Mission Avionics Suite from Marconi Avionics, who also supply the radar for the type. This is the second development aircraft, wearing the new 'hemp' camouflage with 'B'-type roundels. (BAe Manchester)

103. An important asset within the RAF's air defences is the aerial tanker aircraft, which can extend a fighter's range and endurance. The Handley Page Victor K.2s of 57 Sqn. (illustrated refuelling a Tornado F.2 prototype) and 55 Sqn. are to be supplemented from 1983 by nine ex-civil VC.10 airliners converted to tanker configuration. (BAe Warton)

104. The Avro Vulcan bomber is in the final phase of its illustrious service with the RAF. One of the last units to retain the type is 27 Sqn., based at Scampton, flying the strategic reconnaissance version, the Vulcan SR.2 (illustrated). (MoD-Air)

105. The major interdictor aircraft presently based in RAF Germany is the BAe Buccaneer S.2B. Flown by 15 and 16 Sqns. based at Laarbruch, four aircraft are permanently held on quick reaction alert to respond to an enemy threat. This photograph shows two Buccaneers of 15 Sqn. in their low-level wartime environment. In the UK, two squadrons are to be retained for maritime strike duties, equipped with the BAeD Sea Eagle ASM. (MoD-RAFG)

106. The first Panavia Tornado GR.1 for an operational RAF squadron – 9 Sqn., to be based initially at RAF Honington – is seen in this photograph fitted in an engine run-up facility. The Tornadoes will initially replace all the Vulcan squadrons, then the Buccaneer and Jaguar squadrons in RAF Germany, and finally, the UK-based Canberra photo-recce units. (RAF Honington)

107. Four Panavia Tornado GR.1 interdictor-strike aircraft of the Tornado Weapons Conversion Unit, based at RAF Honington. The first crews for the RAF's first operational unit, 9 Sqn., are in the process of training at the time of writing. (RAF Honington)

108. A Jaguar GR.1 of 14 Sqn. landing at Bruggen. The SEPECAT Jaguar GR.1 is the most numerous type of aircraft within RAF Germany at present. Five squadrons are based there: four at Bruggen (14, 17, 20 and 31 Sqns.); and a specialist recce unit (2 Sqn.) at Laarbruch. (MJG)

▲104

▲105 ▼106

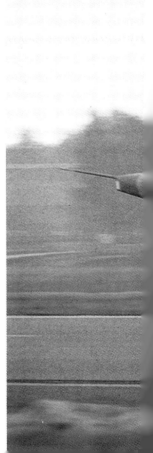

▲109 ▼110

109. The RAF is unique within NATO as the only air force able to field a short take-off, vertical landing (STOVL) close support fighter – the BAe Harrier GR.3. Two units (3 and 4 Sqns.) are based in Germany at Gutersloh, with 1 Sqn. based at Wittering in the UK. This Harrier GR.3 of 4 Sqn. is shown outside its hardened aircraft shelter at Gutersloh. (MJG)

110. In 1981 it was announced that the RAF would procure 60 McDonnell Douglas AV-8B Harrier IIs to replace the Germany-based Harrier GR.3s. In RAF service the AV-8B will be known as the Harrier GR.5. This photograph shows the first full-scale development AV-8B in US Marine Corps markings. The RAF GR.5s will enter service from 1987, and will feature a leading edge root extension (not shown here). (McDonnell Douglas)

111▲

111. In the mid-1960s, the RAF procured 66 Lockheed C-130K Hercules transports. By the late-1970s, 30 aircraft were being 'stretched' to increase their cargo or paratroop capacity. Here, the original Hercules C.1 (left) is seen flying in company with the first 'stretched' Hercules C.3 conversion. (Lockheed-Georgia)

112. The Westland Aérospatiale SA.330 Puma HC.1/2 is the RAF's army support helicopter. The Puma shown here, with an underslung cargo of an Army Land Rover, is from 230 Sqn., based at Gutersloh in Germany. (MoD-RAFG)

113. The long-awaited medium-lift helicopter requirement for the RAF was fulfilled in 1981 with the arrival of the Boeing Vertol Chinook HC.1. The first unit to be equipped was 242 Operation Conversion Unit, based at Odiham (illustrated). Two operational squadrons, 18 and 66 Sqns., are being formed, one of which (18 Sqn.) has deployed to Gutersloh, to complement the Pumas there. (MJG)

112▲ 113▼

▲114 ▼115

114. An early RAF Hawk fitted with Sidewinders, a 30mm gun pod under the fuselage and two external fuel tanks. Although employed in the advanced and weapon training roles, some 72 BAe Hawk T.1s are to be given a limited air defence role, with two AIM-9 Sidewinder air-to-air missiles, for base defence in the event of hostilities. (BAe Kingston)

115. A Canberra PR.9 of 39 Sqn., based at Wyton. This is the last RAF unit equipped with the photo reconnaissance version of the ubiquitous English Electric Canberra. (MoD-Air)

116. The Army's anti-armour helicopter for the 1980s will be the Westland Lynx AH.1, equipped with the Hughes Airborne TOW anti-tank guided weapon. This Lynx is seen firing a TOW missile during final acceptance trials of the system. The Army Air Corps has ordered 114 Lynx to replace the present Scout/SS.11 anti-armour combination. (Westland Helicopters)

117. The Westland/Aérospatiale SA341 Gazelle AH.1 replaced the Sioux in Army Air Corps service in the early 1970s, giving the Army a fast, modern, light observation helicopter. In all, the Army Air Corps has ordered 211 Gazelles. (Westland Helicopters)

116▲ 117▼

▲118

118. The Westland Sea King has been in Fleet Air Arm service all through the 1970s, and looks likely to remain in service in the 1980s. The Sea King HAS.5 version shown here is equipped with MEL Sea Searcher radar, Racal-Decca Tacan (Tactical Air Navigation), new sonobuoy dropping equipment (in addition to the Plessey 195 dunking sonar in evidence) and Marconi Avionics LAPADS data processing equipment. (Westland Helicopters)

119. The Westland Lynx HAS.2 is gradually replacing the Wasp as the small-ship ASW helicopter. Armed with four BAeD Sea Skua anti-ship missiles (shown here), it gives the parent vessel an enhanced anti-ship strike capability. Of the 88 Lynx HAS.2s on order, more than 50 have been delivered. (Westland Helicopters)

120. The Fleet Air Arm fixed-wing element has now centred on the BAe Sea Harrier FRS.1, operating from carriers specially converted or designed to incorporate the ski-jump ramp. To date, the RN has three Sea Harrier units: 899 Sqn., the HQ and Training unit based at Yeovilton; 800 Sqn. based on HMS *Hermes*; and 801 Sqn. on board HMS *Invincible*. This photograph shows representative aircraft from these three squadrons, with 899 Sqn. leading, followed by 800 and 801 Sqns. (BAe Kingston)

121. The 50th TFW at Hahn is to be the first USAFE unit to receive the General Dynamics F-16, the first of which are now in service. This photograph shows a USAF F-16A climbing 'clean', except for the wing-tip mounted AIM-9 Sidewinder missiles. With the multi-staged improvement programme (MSIP) now underway on the F-16, this has become a potent, multi-mission fighter aircraft. (General Dynamics)

122. An F-15 Eagle fully armed with four AIM-9 Side-winders and four AIM-7 Sparrow air-to-air missiles and a drop tank on the centreline.

123. An F-4E of the 86th TFW shown within its hardened aircraft shelter. This photograph was taken at the Tactical Air Meet at Ramstein in 1980. Note the laser designator pod under the engine intake. (R. L. Ward)

124. The reconnaissance variant of the McDonnell Douglas Phantom, the RF-4C, serving with 10th TRW at Alconbury in the UK. A second unit, the 26th TRW is based at Zweibrucken in Germany. (MJG)

122▲

123▲ 124▼

▲ 125

▲ 126 ▼ 127

125. Experience in Vietnam taught the USAF the value of a dedicated anti-SAM radar aircraft, and aircraft so equipped were dubbed 'Wild Weasels'. This McDonnell Douglas F-4G 'Wild Weasel' of the 81st TFS, 52nd TFW is based at Spangdahlem in Germany. Converted from F-4Es, the F-4G is armed with a variety of radar-homing missiles and guided bombs. (USAFE)

126. Until the arrival of the Tornadoes, the General Dynamics F-111 is the only true, all-weather attack aircraft in NATO service. Illustrated is an F-111E of the 20th TFW, based at Upper Heyford in the UK. The F-111F equips the 48th TFW at Lakenheath, also in the UK. (USAFE)

127. Another offshoot of Vietnam experience has been the establishment of 'Aggressor' units in the USAF. These units are equipped with the Northrop F-5E Tiger II fighter, and the aircrews fly them as opponents to other NATO aircraft in exercises. They would be used as air defence aircraft in the event of hostilities. This photograph shows one of the F-5Es of the 527th TFT 'Aggressor' Sqn. at Alconbury. (Chris Buck)

128. In an effort to provide a strong anti-armour air strike force, the USAF conceived what became the A-10 Thunderbolt II attack fighter. Designed to operate at tree-top height and able to survive a large amount of ground anti-aircraft fire, the Fairchild A-10A is an effective part of the USAFE. This A-10 is operated by 81st TFW, based at Bentwaters and Wood-bridge in the UK. Four additional detachments are maintained at Forward Operating Locations in Germany. (Fairchild)

129. The 601st Tactical Control Wing at Sembach in Germany is equipped with 39 Rockwell OV-10A Broncos, an example of which is shown in its original light grey camouflage. They have now adopted the overall 'Lizard' scheme of the A-10 force. (MJG)

128▲ 129▼

▲130

▲131 ▼132

130. The US Army's anti-armour helicopter force is equipped with the Bell AH-1S Improved Cobra gunship, armed with a 30mm Hughes Chain Gun and eight Hughes Airborne TOW anti-tank guided weapons. (MJG)

131. During the 1980s, the AH-1S will be complemented by a number of the larger Hughes AH-64A Apache Advanced Attack Helicopters. One of the development prototypes is illustrated

here. In service they will be armed with sixteen Rockwell Hellfire anti-tank guided weapons and a Hughes 30mm Chain Gun. (Hughes Helicopters)

132. The Sikorsky UH-60A Black Hawk is now entering service with the US Army in the continental USA and the RDF. By the end of the 1980s, this aircraft will be a common sight in Europe. (Sikorsky Aircraft)

▲133

▲134 ▼135

133. The Boeing Vertol CH-47C Chinook, the standard medium-lift helicopter of the US Army. Together with the earlier –A and –B models, the CH-47C is due to be uprated to CH-47D standard, with many improvements (Boeing Vertol)

134. Currently, the Bell UH-1H Iroquois is the standard troop helicopter of the US Army. This aircraft is a UH-1H of the 71st Avn Co of the US Army, assigned to the commander of the Allied Command Europe (ACE) Mobile Force. (MJG)

135. The Bell OH-58A Kiowa is the standard US Army LOH in European service. Many of these are being uprated to OH-58C configuration, while the remainder, some 700 aircraft, are expected to be updated further in the Army Helicopter Improvement Programme recently announced. (MJG)